AGILE ACCESSIBILITY HANDBOOK

www.amplifypublishing.com

Agile Accessibility Handbook

For more information, please contact:
Amplify Publishing, an imprint of Mascot Books
620 Herndon Parkway, Suite 320
Herndon, VA 20170
info@amplifypublishing.com

Library of Congress Control Number: 2020908348

CPSIA Code: PRV0720A
ISBN-13: 978-1-64543-477-1

Printed in the United States

To all the pioneers of accessibility technology who came before us, and the current-day practitioners who will make their vision a reality.

DYLAN BARRELL

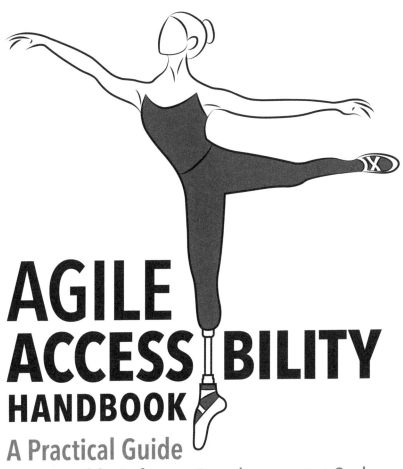

AGILE ACCESSIBILITY
HANDBOOK

A Practical Guide
to Accessible Software Development at Scale

CONTENTS

Foreword

At Deque, we have worked with dozens of organizations, from the largest companies that belong to the Fortune 500, to some small organizations who outsource most of their development. In the process, we have worked with hundreds of development teams and thousands of developers. Our work has encompassed everything from arms-length assess-and-report engagements (where the developers receive a "report" of all the accessibility issues and some generic instructions on how to fix them) to long-term engagements (where we were embedded in the development teams and sat in the same cube rows or collaborative working spaces with access to their source code repository, their ticket tracking systems, testing and build environments, etc.).

In the process, we have learned—sometimes the hard way—what works and what does not for remediation jobs on large, existing code bases and for teaching these teams to become independent.

We also develop our own software and have been using agile development processes in one form or another for almost a decade. When we develop software with a user interface, we develop it to be "accessible by default," and we will not ship any software with known serious accessibility issues that we can control. This has taught us valuable principles for developing accessible software in an agile environment, and we teach these principles to our customers.

Deque also facilitates an "accessibility user group" meeting, where the executives in charge of accessibility at large organizations can share their experiences with each other. We have learned from these discussions; they have driven the development of some new practices and helped us to refine existing ones.

One of the most valuable advantages of the agile development process is that the process itself is not seen as something fixed, but as an artifact that is to be improved as part of the process. I have presented in this book the best practices as we know them today, but we continue to improve and refine them and identify new or better ones. I hope you will learn something from this book, but I hope even more that it will inspire you to teach us something, too.

The book is inspired by the one that first introduced me to agile development back in the late nineties—*Extreme Programming Explained* (first edition). In particular, section two, which introduces the practices required for extreme programming.

This book is intended to be read by three audiences: People involved in running or setting up a central accessibility function within an organization, the executives that set software development and business priorities, and the people involved in the agile teams that are delivering the software to meet those business objectives.

Executives should read the entire book so they understand the challenges that stand in the way of sustainable accessibility, the organizational structures required to make the necessary transition, and the impact this will have on the work performed by the different groups.

The central accessibility function should read the book so that they understand what their role is in making the changes happen, the resources that they must create and maintain, and the support they must provide to the teams doing the work.

The developers need to understand the changes they must make to their development processes and what they can expect from the rest of the organization to help them make this happen.

Sections 1 and 2 provide an overview of the problems that need to be solved. Section 3 details the role of the central accessibility function and the practices that can help to make their work successful. Section 4 lays out the team practices that help teams to make accessible software development efficient and effective.

At the end of the book, I have provided a glossary of terms that will help readers to understand some of the technical terms that may not be familiar to them. Development team members can find accessibility jargon (e.g. WCAG) defined in the glossary, and accessibility experts can find technical terms (e.g. Sprint) explained.

1

What Does "Agile" Mean?

Agile is a term that is overused almost to the point of being useless, but I have my own interpretation. For the purposes of this book, I mean specifically the software development and deployment process where:

1. Software is being constantly released, weekly, monthly, or in some cases, multiple times daily. This is important, because "traditional" accessibility testing is impossible to do in this sort of environment; and

2. The teams are committed to continuous improvement of their practices, and these practices are designed to make the team more efficient, allow them to gather data from users, and respond to this data with the aim of producing software that satisfies customer and market needs and provides an excellent user experience.

These two principles have a lot of follow-on requirements that teams must learn to meet, including,

1. The need for a team to be self-sufficient and able to make decisions in real time; and
2. The need to automate as much as humanly possible to avoid costly and slow release cycles.

If your agile methodology does not embrace these principles or your organization still practices waterfall software development, then the benefits to your development process will be diminished, but they will still provide some value. The more technical team practices will still be applicable as-is, as will most of the the transformation practices.

Why is
Accessibility Hard?

Accessibility, at its core, is quite simple. It basically comes down to three principles[1]:

1. Can all your users, with the abilities and senses that they possess, perceive the infor-

---

[1] Those of you familiar with the Web Content Accessibility Guidelines might ask yourselves where the fourth principle, "robustness," is. I have not forgotten it; I believe that it is an explicitly technical principle that does not add much to the understanding of accessibility, and have therefore excluded it for simplicity.

mation your application presents to them? For example, can they "see" the meaning of the little icon button with an image of a pen inside it?

2. Can your users, with their specific input device or assistive technology, operate all the controls within your application's user interface? For example, if your application supports the operation of a button through touching the screen, does it also allow that button to be operated through a keyboard and a voice command?

3. Can your users understand the information and the user interface controls? For example, if the application requires the creation of a password with constraints, are those constraints clearly communicated in a way that allows the user to complete the task without undue difficulty or an unreasonable degree of intellectual skill?

Given that the principles are this simple, why do development teams made up of the best and the brightest graduates of the best schools in the world routinely develop and ship software that is horribly inaccessible, shutting out large swathes of potential users and customers?

2.1 The Bubble

Current best practice in software user interface development calls for personas, wireframes, prototypes, user testing, user observation and discovery, and whatever the latest fashion is in UI design (as of this writing, flat material design is a big thing). These practices are supposed to discover hidden needs and common use cases and result in simple, minimally viable designs and easy-to-use interfaces.

The personas that are created can be seen as very diverse. They include working mothers, people of different ethnicities, stay-at-home dads, remote workers, people who are gay, queer, genderfluid, etc.

The agile team members (most in their mid-to-late twenties) attend usability testing sessions to observe for themselves how the participants use their solution. They have sessions to analyze the difficulties certain participants found, empathizing with the user to try to understand the root causes and come up with potential solutions. They create wireframes and prototypes to attempt to solve these usability problems and iterate until they have nailed the problem. "The Uber of . . .?" is written on the wall of the team workspace in big, bold letters to remind everyone of the big picture goal.

All of this is designed to take the team out of its bubble, away from the natural tendency to

---

[2] Insert the appropriate product category here

use their own experiences as a filter or a guide for the product they are creating.

The team may have gone to great lengths to avoid the "white male bias" that is all too prevalent in technology, but they are still blind to another hidden bias: they are all healthy, highly intelligent, physically fit and capable, mostly twenty-somethings with almost no impairments to their abilities. They have (for the most part) zero experience with people with disabilities, and they have little experience with older people.

Put another way, most of the people on these teams are living in an "able-bodied bubble" and they don't know it.

The following is an abstracted—but very representative—conversation I have had many times with developers, product owners, testers, UX designers, and executives as I have worked with customers or interacted with visitors to the Deque booth at conferences and trade shows:

ME: Hi. My name is Dylan. What is your name?

MARY: Hi. I'm Mary. What does Deque do?

ME: Do you know what accessibility is?

I can see the gears turning in Mary's head as she tries to figure out the correct answer (as any self-respecting developer would expect to be able to do).

MARY: Well, yes, it's about making sure people can get to your application . . .?

ME: Well, not really. Accessibility is about making sure that people with disabilities can use your application.

The gear-churning goes into overdrive as this statement sinks in, so I continue unabated . . .

ME: Have you ever thought about how a blind person would use your application?

Mary looks at me quizzically, a wry smile on her face; she thinks I'm punking her.

I whip out my iPhone and with three presses on the home button, turn on Voiceover and put the iPhone up to her ear so she can hear it. I have it turned down to what most blind users would consider an "irritatingly slow" speech speed so that "light-dependent" people can understand it.

MARY: Oh, cool, did you write that software?

ME: No, that software is called a screen reader, and you have it on your phone, too. What we do is we help developers figure out how to make their applications work with that software so that people with disabilities can use their applications. How do you think a blind person could (air quotes) see an image?

Gears churning . . .

ME: Well, it's actually very simple, you just have to add a textual description of that image and attach it to the image in the appropriate way. Then, the screen reader will read it out, giving the blind user some understanding of what a sighted user would see in the image . . .

The conversation goes on, and there is always a genuine interest in trying to understand more about this "new" topic: How do I make my application usable by blind people? Where can I learn about this? Why have I not heard about this before? Sometimes I hear something along the lines of, "Oh yeah, we got sued once, and we had this company come in and help us fix our Website," or "Yeah, is that Section 508 or something? We had an external company create a VPAT for us once."

2.2 The Empathy Gap

This is what I call the empathy gap; it is a blind spot that exists in 99% of all development teams. It leads to unconscious bias in the development of user interfaces and serves as a barrier to acquiring the skills and knowledge necessary to do accessible software development. If you want your teams to develop software that is "accessible by default," then removing this block (thereby increasing their motivation to learn) is the first and most important thing you need to do.

The empathy gap starts to be filled when someone (like Mary) becomes aware of these groups of people who they are unintentionally and unnecessarily excluding. However, there is more to closing the gap than that. Once someone realizes blind people can actually use a touch device using a screen reader, there is still a long way to go before they understand how blind people use that screen reader and what the capabilities of the screen reader are.

Closing the empathy gap acts as a motivator that drives people to want to learn about people with disabilities, how they use assistive technologies, and what this means for software development teams.

This empathy gap is exacerbated by the fact that, for many user interface interaction patterns, the group of professionals referred to as "human computer interaction professionals" or "user experience designers" has compiled a rich collection of best practices and principles that application developers can fall back on. These have been developed over time and tested using research techniques like eye tracking, click tracking, observation, analytics, and the like. There is very little comparable information for people with different abilities and users of assistive technologies.

This lack of well understood best practices means that developers have to start answering questions like:

1. How does a blind user scan the page?
2. How does a blind user identify the important parts of a user interface?
3. How does a user of voice recognition scroll to the information that is "below the fold?"

Some of the practices listed later in the book are designed to systematically fill the empathy gap in your agile teams and motivate them to learn the answers to these questions and more.

2.3 The Skills Gap

Once a team has begun to understand the different disabilities and mechanisms that are used to accommodate for these disabilities with assistive technologies, they then realize that they do not know how to ensure that *their* applications will be usable with these assistive technologies. They also still need to learn what they need to do to enable ease of use for users with disabilities for which no special assistive technology is available—like users with cognitive disabilities, repetitive stress injuries (keyboard only users), color-blind users, and deaf users.

Closing the empathy gap helps the team to understand that a screen reader user scans the page by asking the screen reader (using keyboard or gesture commands) to expose various semantic structures—such as headings and regions that they can easily navigate around the page using commands to jump to particular structures, like the next heading or the next table. The team then needs to determine the answers to questions like, "What do I need to do to make sure my application is exposing all the right structures and information so that the screen reader user will be able to successfully navigate the user interface?"

The answer to these sorts of questions is the skills gap. Any organization that is serious about accessibility must take systematic steps to give the agile team members both up-front training and on-demand resources that allow them to learn the appropriate markup attributes, technologies, and APIs, as well as allowing them to find and understand the best practices for solving particular user interface and usability challenges.

A person with a visual disability demonstrates using a braille keyboard attached to their computer. The pins move up and down as the user interface changes to be able to represent the currently spoken screen reader text.

Transformation Practices

If your organization has been developing software for a significant amount of time, it is highly likely that you did not start out using an agile methodology. Your organization probably went through some form of agile transformation or (more recently perhaps) a digital transformation. You probably hired some consultants to manage this process, and they probably brought in a bevy of agile coaches, trainers, and scrum masters to help your organization.

Successfully adopting agile accessibility will require a large amount of change in behavior throughout the organization. If you want to be successful, you will need to manage the agile accessibility transformation process. You will need to bring in the missing skills and knowledge and find ways to support teams as they go through the process of adopting new behaviors.

The practices covered in the next chapter in the book are designed to help the organization manage this agile accessibility transformation and ensure that it is successful, even in the face of active or passive resistance in the agile teams or in the managers who are responsible for setting the priorities of these teams.

The Transformation Practices are designed to help your organization manage the agile accessibility transformation. Successfully implementing these practices is the prerequisite for successful agile accessibility. That is not to say that you cannot have some teams successfully adopt agile accessibility, but without these practices, you will find it very difficult (if not impossible) to get consistent adoption and execution across the organization, and you will see a degradation in the abilities over time through team member attrition.

At the end of the day, becoming accessible involves change in large parts of the organization; this change will not happen if it is not motivated, measured, and managed.

3.1 Practice: Create a
Central Accessibility Team

Every organization that has successfully scaled accessibility (agile or otherwise) has always started with a central accessibility team. The difference in an agile environment is that this central team is not responsible for doing accessibility (as was often the case before agile), but rather for helping the agile teams learn to do accessibility within their agile process. In short, it is the job of the central accessibility team to manage the transformation to sustainable agile accessibility.

The central team's primary responsibilities are:

1. Educate executives on the business case for accessibility and obtain executive buy-in;
2. Create and manage the corporate accessibility policy;
3. Create and maintain the learning resources for the entire organization, including (but not limited to) agile teams, customer support, and procurement;
4. Create, gather, and report the metrics that are being used to measure the transformation and to identify the opportunities for more coaching, training, and tools. This responsibility includes performing spot audits of newly-released content and presenting the results back to the teams during their retrospectives;
5. Keep abreast of developments in accessibility (including understanding accessibility for new platforms [like virtual reality, speech inputs, etc.], improvements in tools and new

or improved best practices) and then planning the steps to incorporate the acquired knowledge into the organization's processes at the appropriate time;

6. Create and maintain the organization's accessibility standards (interpreting the industry guidelines and standards and applying them to the organization's technologies) and the selection and configuration of the tools being used by the various teams; and

7. Provide the pool of accessibility coaches and other shared resources that are required during the transition.

3.2 Practice: Obtain Executive Buy-In

The motherhood and apple pie of accessibility transformation is that you need executive buy-in. If you have managed to put together a central team, then you have the basis for getting the right sort of executive buy-in.

Ultimately, the CEO needs to buy in to accessibility, or it will constantly be overridden by competing priorities; however, starting at the top is not always practical and is often not enough.

Buy-in is required from all the levels of management in the compliance, marketing, and IT/

development parts of the organization, because any one of these could become an impediment to success.

The ultimate goal here is to ensure that none of the executives will seriously challenge the implementation of the policy that is instrumental to making accessibility stick.

The ways that you achieve this buy-in will depend to a large degree on your organizational priorities, but there are three business cases that you can use to help your efforts:

1. The business opportunity represented by households with a disability. The numbers that are of interest here are:

    i. 20% of people in the United States have a disability, and improvements in usability (or falling behind the competition) represent a major portion of the market;

    ii. $490 million is the after-tax disposable income of adults with a disability in the United States (as of 2019). This is comparable in size to the African American or Hispanic market segments; and

iii. $10.3 billion is the e-commerce market size for accessibility.

2. The number of disability-related lawsuits increased by 181% in 2019 alone, and the cost of responding to a lawsuit (independent of the settlement costs) is $350,000. This does not take into account the cost of brand damage or future lawsuits; and

3. Accessibility is a human right, it is the right thing to do, and it probably aligns with the organization's values and its desire to improve digital user experiences.

Find the right opportunities to get in front of the executives and pitch these cases to them.

3.3 Practice: Create and Enforce an Accessibility Policy

Once you have enough executive support, you need to ensure that this support gets into the organization's official policy and the risks are exposed and managed appropriately.

Understand how your organization manages risk. If you are in a regulated industry, this will be relatively easy, and the attention to risks that show up in the system will be at the appropriate level.

Your policy should be written in such a way that it minimizes the loopholes that will inevitably be exploited by savvy managers.

Some attributes of successful policies are to:

1. Require all digital properties to be registered in a central repository;

2. Require all digital properties to report their accessibility (the format of a VPAT is a good starting point) and treat non-reporting as tantamount to critical defects in critical business flows;

3. Create a place in your risk management system for registering the specific accessibility defects with their impact and a timeline for remediation. Tie accessibility risks to existing mechanisms for escalation; and

4. Produce regular reports for delivery to the chief compliance officer and the CEO, summarizing the trends and highlighting the business areas that are not addressing their risk in the appropriate way.

The rest of this book is dedicated to the carrots, but having the policy stick can be very useful, especially when dealing with intransigent managers.

The way that this policy is enforced—and the perception of the central accessibility team in the enforcement of this policy—can be instrumental in the success of the program. The central accessibility team needs to be viewed as a helping hand with useful resources and advice to help the teams achieve accessibility. This can be undermined if the central team is also the face of policy enforcement. Try to locate the enforcement function in the compliance department and the rest of the central accessibility team within a different function such as IT, software development, or the office of the CIO.

The central accessibility team may help teams provide data to compliance but it must never be seen as the cop or a scuttlebutt.

.

3.4 Practice: Report on Your Accessibility Transformation

In order to manage the adoption of accessibility at your organization, you will need to have senior management buy-in; you will need to provide management with periodic reporting that is easy for them to understand and allows them to recognize what is working well and what needs attention. This means you should create a dashboard report that surfaces this information across all areas of the business.

Organizations adopt accessibility for a variety of reasons. Some organizations are proactive and attempt to create delightful experiences and win market share. Some organizations are reactive and respond to a complaint or a consent decree. The way your organization reports on the accessibility program will need to reflect the underlying motivation.

Regardless of the motivation, your dashboard should be designed to help you measure how your process is changing over time and to measure the direction of that change. Adopting accessibility is about adopting new behaviors which, in turn, leads to a change in the desired outcomes. This means that early on in your process, you should focus on a dashboard that allows you to measure the adoption of new behaviors.

A mid-sized regional bank we work with has a team responsible for creating and maintaining tools for their development teams to use in their testing and continuous integration pipeline. As a part of their agile transformation, the team also assists development teams in learning how to adopt and use automation. They have built an analytics dashboard that shows how the use and adoption of the automation tools is changing over time. When they added automated accessibility testing to this tool set, they saw an opportunity to also measure the adoption of the automated accessibility testing as an early indicator of successful accessibility implementation.

In a large accessibility remediation project that needs to meet a specific deadline, the dashboard should include some sort of overall effort metrics as well as the effect of those efforts over time. The goal of this report is to predict whether the deadline is likely to be met. A variation of a "burndown" report is a good candidate to consider for this purpose. Seeing the overall effort at the enterprise-level is useful, but you will also need to drill down to see how individual teams, products, applications, or sites are doing. A good dashboard should allow for viewing the progress in ways that align with how the organization is managing the development and/or remediation effort. This provides updates to the executives in charge of these teams and identifies teams that could benefit from additional support from the central team.

Simple indicators of health status, like red, green, and yellow (with appropriate accessible equivalents), can help to communicate complex information efficiently and are great tools for high-level dashboards. Once you start to get down to the individual team, application, or website, you will need to answer questions like, "What is the cause of the change?" This will require you to be able to answer questions like, "What changed?" A high-level aggregate score that did not change between two releases (but was expected to) could be masking the fact that a large number of issues were remediated and a large number of new issues were introduced. There could be some new pages, new functionality, or a change in the scope of what was being included in the report.

Your reporting system should be able to answer

questions like, "Which pages/views are new?" "Which pages/views were removed?" and "What, if anything, has changed on the pages/views that are common between the two reporting dates?" These questions will need to be answered at aggregate levels (an entire application or site) as well as at the level of individual pages/views and components.

One of our customers has a report that shows the engagement level of the teams. They differentiate between teams that are still remediating and teams that are trying to ensure that their new content and functionality is accessible. This is reported as "team maturity."

3.5 Practice: Give the Teams Accessibility Coaches

Agile teams need training in the skills required to successfully implement accessible software development. This training can take many forms, from intense in-person, multi-day workshops to on-demand online learning.

Intense training workshops give team members a jump-start in the basic technical knowledge. When the team starts to exercise this knowledge, they will make mistakes, misinterpret some of the information, forget some aspects of the implementation, or encounter problems that go beyond the basics. Practical experience is required to cement the theoretical knowledge and to fill in the gaps in recall that all of us experience when learning new skills.

Accessibility coaches can help teams identify the areas where they need to reinforce their training, help answer difficult implementation questions, and provide coaching on some of the finer points or tradeoffs between different implementation decisions.

In the initial phases, accessibility coaches attend many of the agile activities where decisions on implementation are made. This includes backlog grooming meetings, design reviews, sprint planning, daily standup, and retrospectives.

During these meetings, they encourage the agile team to consider accessibility concerns, remember to use existing automation libraries and tools in the development process, and include accessibility testing and implementation in their planning estimates and tests. They help team members think through the various approaches to inclusive design and present the results of the spot audits and the accessibility testing during retrospectives.

The use of the term "coach" is explicit. It makes it clear to everyone where the responsibility for doing the work lies. Coaches do not make the free throws, throw the strikes, or score the goals. Coaches help the players practice the skills they need and interact with other team members in ways that make the team successful.

3.6 Practice: Execute on an Ongoing Empathy Campaign

To become an organization where inclusive design and accessible software development is the norm, your organization will need to systematically eliminate the empathy gap. This can only happen if the central accessibility team maintains an ongoing campaign to achieve it.

The central accessibility team should create a schedule of activities, to be held on an ongoing basis, the aim of which is to systematically build empathy for people with disabilities.

These activities should target new and existing employees to build and reinforce empathy continually. While most of the targets for these activities should be agile software development team members, it is essential to secure participation by senior managers and executives, too.

The following lists some activities that have shown success at Deque and our customers:

1. Events where persons with disabilities demonstrate using the company's applications with assistive technologies;
2. Events where participants play games that simulate disabilities;
3. Posters, flyers, success stories, and other motivational marketing; and
4. Hackathons or hack weeks with an accessibility focus.

In addition to scheduling and holding these events, the central accessibility team should make themselves and their resources available to support team empathy events. They should create stickers that teams can place on their laptops. It is very encouraging to show up at a meeting with a team and see accessibility stickers on the backs of laptops. It allows teams and team members to show their support and helps drive awareness.

The Global Accessibility Awareness Day (GAAD), founded by Jennison Asuncion and Joe Devon, is a once-a-year opportunity to highlight accessibility in a very intensive way. Held in the middle of May, it is celebrated all over the world. Your employees can attend events in person or online; it is a great opportunity to host and/or participate in events in your area. Visit https://globalaccessibilityawarenessday.org to find events and to register your own. Hosting events that are open to the public is also a great way to recruit employees who are motivated and can help to drive change within your organization.

3.7 Practice: Publish Learning Resources and Bulletins

Intensive training can help to jumpstart the knowledge of agile team members. We recommend making bootcamp style in-person training available to the teams. We also recommend including some form of accessibility training in the on-boarding training of all employees involved in software development or client-facing roles.

Most people will absorb some fraction of the training and will benefit from resources that they can access at the time they are required to exercise the new skills. Developers in particular like to learn as they implement functionality. Stack Overflow is an example of a system that supports this "on-demand" learning.

The quality of accessibility information available on Stack Overflow and on the Internet in general is varied, both in terms of validity and how up-to-date it is. This can lead to a lot of wasted time as team members research solutions and implement partial or out-of-date solutions.

Providing access to a quality knowledge base of up-to-date accessibility information, examples, and courses can mitigate this problem. In addition, reinforcing the awareness of this knowledge base will support the behavior of using it as the resource of first resort.

To eliminate the frustration and false starts that result from following bad or out-of-date accessibility advice, license or create a set of resources that document known and proven solutions to various accessibility issues such as:

1. Procedures for testing different types of content or applications;
2. Technical solutions to specific UI component implementations and user interface patterns; and
3. Documentation on best practices.

There are commercial solutions with knowledge bases and online courses that include tests, examples, and tools, but very successful accessibility programs have also taken a low-cost approach to this. One of our customers keeps a single Web page with links to information that has been gathered and curated over time. This page serves as a starting point for teams when they're looking for a solution or some learning resources.

Sending out regular information bulletins that highlight new topical accessibility insights, specific techniques, and notices of upcoming industry events can help to keep accessibility top-of-mind for the development teams. If you do this, embed links to the knowledge base in

these updates to maintain and increase awareness of the resource.

Empathy lab participants write their names using a
Braille template and then try to read them with their
eyes closed.

4

Team Practices

In my opinion, one of the most valuable aspects of the agile approach to software development is the commitment to continuous improvement. Sprint retrospectives are one of the most valuable practices that support this continuous improvement. Teams that do this well have metrics that they inspect and track over time, identify the things that are going well and identify and address deficiencies or problems.

Changes that get identified in these meetings can be modifications to practices to ensure that they are actually achieving the outcomes for which they were adopted in the first place. In order to do this, all team members need to have a thorough understanding of the intended outcome and/or goal of every practice, and the team has to regularly evaluate each practice for its effectiveness within their team.

I have structured the following nine team practices to make the goal of each explicit so that teams that adopt them can evaluate their effectiveness continually.

As with any new practice, your team should try to adopt it "as-is" so you can get experience with it before attempting to modify it using your own insights. However, after some experience has been gained, I highly encourage teams to experiment with new variants or new practices in the attempt to efficiently achieve the target outcomes.

As is the case with many agile practices, some advantage can be gained by implementing individual practices; however, the full benefit can only be seen when all practices are adopted and implemented well together.

4.1 Practice: Attend and Host Empathy Events

GOALS:

1. To help team members better understand what it is like to live with different disabilities; and

2. To help team members understand how users with disabilities use assistive technologies.

PRACTICE DESCRIPTION: Hold events that simulate for the team members what it is like to have a specific disability and how this might affect the use of technology. Hold events where people with disabilities demonstrate the use of assistive technologies and/or attempt to use the team's application with an assistive technology.

EXAMPLE: When first learning that blind people use a screen reader that reads out the content of the user interface and a keyboard to navigate the page, Web developers often mistakenly believe that every textual element on a Web page must be tab-focusable; they will start to place `tabindex=0` on every element. This reaction is based on a misunderstanding of how screen readers work as well as a failure to understand how a browser can be controlled with a keyboard. Making every element tab focusable results in a Web page that is less usable by keyboard-only users; it also does nothing to improve the experience of a screen reader user.

By bringing a screen reader user in to demonstrate the many ways that they can navigate a Web page, the team will learn that the `tabindex` is not required. They will also begin to understand the importance of semantic markup, good heading structure, and landmarks. They will start to be able to use heuristics to predict what good experiences might be for screen reader and keyboard-only users.

Examples of empathy events:

1. Dining in the dark, where the group eats an entire dinner in complete darkness. This can be enhanced by including a blind person, who will, for once, be at an advantage;

2. Empathy lab, a dedicated location with a collection of activities made up of devices, exercises, and games that team members can participate in to simulate the difficulties that various disabilities impose. The activities can simulate physical conditions such as hearing impairment, vision loss, aging, or motor impairment. The exercises can force the participants to use accommodations similar to those used by people with disabilities to achieve the goal or win the game. The aim of using an empathy lab is

to motivate the need for learning new skills and to jumpstart the understanding of how people with disabilities experience the world and technology;

3. Assistive technology show-and-tell booths, where people with disabilities show how they use the technologies to overcome their disabilities and also how bad implementations can block these technologies or make them more difficult to use; and

4. Device impairment, where a computer or touch device is modified to remove one form of output and/or input, forcing the user to use a modality commonly used by a person with a disability. This can be as simple as unplugging the mouse, replacing the keyboard with a single-switch device, or removing all color to simulate color blindness.

4.2 Practice: Include Disabilities in UX Design

When the ADA was enacted, the industries most affected by the law at the time (builders, landlords, and cities) complained about the burden that it would place on them and the economy. One of the requirements that flowed out of the ADA was the implementation of the ramps at the corners of streets known as "curb cuts." Curb cuts (and other related ramps) have allowed parents with strollers complete and easy access to all aspects of our cities, where previously they had to struggle to navigate the sidewalks and the entrances to buildings. Curb cuts allow skateboarders, bicyclers, and rollerbladers to easily navigate the sidewalks, keeping them out of the streets and safer from bad interactions with traffic. None of these benefits were anticipated when the ADA was enacted, but the result is cities that are more usable by everyone.

In the accessibility industry, this is known as "The Curb Cut Principle," and it applies equally to online and digital experiences. Inclusive design is the practice that achieves this in the digital world.

The question for the teams becomes, "How do we learn to do inclusive design?" While there are books that focus just on the practices of inclusive design, including users with disabilities in design and UX research goes a long way towards achieving many of the same outcomes.

GOAL: To make thinking about users with disabilities an integral part of the user interface and user experience design process so that the final product works better for all users.

PRACTICE DESCRIPTION: Create a collection of attributes that represent a particular type of disability. We call these "particularities," because they represent a particular way in which a person with that disability differs from someone without the disability. In all other ways, they are exactly the same. Your team can then use these particularities to evaluate the UX/UI to determine how that would affect use.

If your team employs user personas, each particularity can be added to an existing persona, or the personas can be modified using the particularities. This practice is also known as creating "inclusive personas."

EXAMPLE: The image following shows an inclusive persona used by a fitness tracking device company.

Meet Lucy (as an inclusive person)

"I want to still be able to access my tracker data when I don't have my phone on me."

Age
33

Occupation
Event Organizer

Family
Long-term relationship (no kids)

Location
Chicago, IL

Particularity

Lucy was born blind and relies on screen readers and haptic audio feedback

Goals

- Figue out what her ideal steps-per-day goal should be

- Find more ways to be motivated to be healthy, using the tracker

- Find a tracker thas has really good audio and haptic feedback

Frustrations

- Sometimes too busy to remember to charge it and loses steps

- The wristbands come loose over time and don't feel as nice

- When she wants to see her tracker data, she HAS to use the app

This inclusive persona describes Lucy, a thirty-three-year-old event organizer who has very normal goals related to the fitness tracking device—she wants to use it to motivate her to be more active and healthy. She also wants a tracker that has good haptic and audio feedback, because she just happens to be blind, and most fitness tracking devices have output modalities that require sight.

Incorporating particularities into the personas allows you to identify specific frustrations; in this case, Lucy is forced to always use the app when looking at her data, which means that she often cannot easily access it while working out.

Another approach to achieve similar outcomes is to consider versions of your personas with "temporary disabilities" that may be caused by situational changes or temporary health events. Using a cell phone in bright sunlight is similar to having low vision; using a cell phone in a noisy restaurant is similar to having a hearing disability; having a broken arm is a temporary situation that has the same effect as a similar permanent motor impairment. Microsoft has published some excellent material in this area that can be found on their inclusive design Web site, https://www.microsoft.com/design/inclusive/.

4.3 Practice: Communicate Intent with Accessibility Design Annotation

User interface and user experience designers create very robust models of their designs in their heads that include a lot of information that is essential to implementing an accessible experience. Many designers do not know that much of this information needs to be communicated to the rest of the team in order to implement the design in an accessible way. They also do not know which information needs to be communicated to the rest of the team in order to ensure that the user interface is accessible. This leads to developers either making up the missing information (e.g., adding their own image text alternative) or simply omitting that semantic or information completely because they are not sure what to apply. Our analyses have shown that up to 70%[3] of accessibility issues can be avoided by systematically communicating the necessary information to the entire development team.

GOAL: Communicate all of the necessary accessibility design intent to the team so that designs can be turned into accessible applications, and this accessibility can be tested and validated efficiently.

---

[3] This number is calculated in different ways, all arriving at around the same number. Some of these calculations have been done with the data from accessibility audits done by Deque over many years, and then classifying each issue as to whether better direction from the designs could have avoided it. A more direct approach is to categorize all WCAG 2 A and AA as to whether design should have a major influence on the success of the criterion. When you do this, 67% of the success criteria fall into the "major influence" category.

PRACTICE DESCRIPTION: Train all team members to expect user experience and user interface designers to provide them with all the following information for a new or modified user interface design:

1. The role of every element in the user interface, whether interactive or not. This includes communicating the role of regions of information and groups of controls. For example, if your design has a group of navigational controls at the top and some information in the footer, indicate where the main content begins and ends, then mark this up in a wireframe or design comp so that everyone knows what those regions are;

2. The states that every user interface element can take on and the text description of those states. For example, if your application has an order workflow with many steps, ensure that the states for the future steps,

the current step, and the completed steps are identified and described;

3. All of the discrete values that the elements can take on and the text description of those values. For example, if a section of the user interface can be expanded and collapsed, describe these different states in text;

4. The name of every element, region, or group of controls in the user interface. For example, if your interface has a main section of content and then some supplemental content, identify the content regions and describe them in text;

5. A complete description of the interaction for each interactive element and its surrounding elements, including all inputs for all supported devices and how this affects the focus, the states, and the values of the interactive element and related elements;

6. The intended order in which elements should be encountered and read on the page (reading order/focus order); and

7. The minimum sizes of all interactive elements at all device or browser sizes.

Different teams may use different ways to communicate their user experience designs in such a way that developers and testers can implement and validate the functionality. We do not dictate *how* this communication takes place, but rather *that* it takes place. We have seen teams use white boards and cell phone photos appended to JIRA tickets; we have also seen teams use high-resolution Photoshop comps with annotations built in. Choose the mechanism that works best for your team.

There are also many different ways to make the annotations; the important thing is that your team agrees on an annotation convention and uses it consistently.

EXAMPLE: The image following shows a very simple player toolbar component with three buttons–a previous track button, a play/pause button, and a next track button. One could imagine this widget being used in different scenarios: Sometimes on its own, and others with a real-time frequency histogram or a control that shows the progress of the track being played.

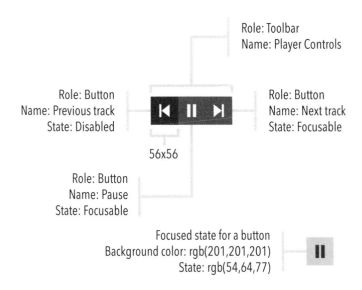

Role: Toolbar
Name: Player Controls

Role: Button
Name: Previous track
State: Disabled

Role: Button
Name: Next track
State: Focusable

56x56

Role: Button
Name: Pause
State: Focusable

Focused state for a button
Background color: rgb(201,201,201)
State: rgb(54,64,77)

Interaction for the role=button

Keyboard SPACE or ENTER equals click
Disabled buttons cannot receive focus
Disabled buttons do not respond to a click/touch

Interaction for the entire component

When on first track: disable "previous track" button
When on last track: disable "next track" button and hide the "play" button
When not playing: display the "play" button and hide the "pause" button
After clicking "play," place focus on the "pause" button
After clicking "pause," place focus on the "play" button

This image has been annotated with a lot of the necessary accessibility information.

The first thing to note is that the role of every element has been specified. This includes the role of the toolbar itself, which is, of course, "toolbar." This may seem at first to be superfluous, but we have seen situations where a designer has intended for something to be a button, and they believe that their design comp clearly shows a button, only to be implemented by a `<div>` element with a click handler or an anchor element styled to look like a button.

Second, the name of each element has been specified. Once again, this may seem obvious given that the toolbar buttons are all image buttons, but one of the most common accessibility violations we find during testing is a button that has no text name at all, or is simply the name of the image file. Having the designer specify the name allows for more consistent usage of terminology throughout the user experience and also allows the testers to validate something that is not visible through automation, thereby making it more difficult to miss a regression where this hidden text is changed or removed.

Third, each of the different states of the buttons has been specified. There is a disabled state (slightly darker gray background), the focusable state, and the focused state (light gray background at the bottom of the image). There are no values in this design comp, but you could easily imagine that the number of previous or next tracks might be a value and how this might be annotated.

Fourth, you will notice that the interaction of each element and of the elements within the toolbar is described. Of great importance are things like what happens to focus when the pause/play button is pressed. Focus management is one of the most frequent accessibility issues in Web applications and can lead to applications that are very difficult for blind users to use; content changes, appears, or disappears without informing the user at all, leading to the belief that the application is not responding to the user's input.

In this specific component, it is important because it would be easy for developers to implement this not as one button, but as two buttons whose visibility is toggled based on the component's internal state. Specifying what happens with the focus allows the testers (or, more likely, the automated tests) to validate that focus does, in fact, get maintained correctly during this state transition.

Finally, the size of the objects is specified, which, in this case (because everything is square), is a very simple annotation.

> **EXAMPLE:** The images following show a design comp without and then with additional accessibility annotations that are important for keyboard and screen reader users. The user interface shown is the axe browser extension, which allows for testing Web applications for accessibility issues.

The second image shows annotations that provide the information about where the focus should go and in what order the interactive elements should receive focus when a keyboard or screen reader user tabs into the application and then continues to tab through the user interface. Tabbing should skip over the non-focusable elements.

The third annotation shows the reading order of the content. Note that the reading order and the focus order are aligned. This is important to avoid breaking the meaning of the content in the application (which can inadvertently occur if there is a mismatch between these two orders).

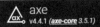

axe
v4.4.1 (**axe-core** 3.5.1)

What you're analyzing   ⌄

https://www.google.com/   Upgrade to axe Pro to analyze an individual component

All issues found 16 ▾   ⇄ Save results   ↺ Run again

Required ARIA attributes must be provided   1

Page must have means to bypass repeated blocks   1

Images must have alternate text   1

Document must have one main landmark   1

Page must contain a level-one heading   1

Required ARIA attributes must be provided   « ‹ 1 of 1 › »
</> Inspect Node ↻ Highlight

Issue description   Impact: **critical**
Ensures elements with ARIA roles have all required ARIA attributes   ↗Learn more

Element location

.gLFyf

Element source

```
<input class="gLFyf gsfi" maxlength="2048" name="q" type="text"
jsaction="paste:puy29d" aria-autocomplete="both" aria-haspopup="false"
autocapitalize="off" autocomplete="off" autocorrect="off" autofocus=""
role="combobox" spellcheck="false" title="Search" value="" aria-label="Search"
data-ved="0ahUKEwi0rpye3Z_pAhXTbc0KHauLBC4Q39UDCAY">
```

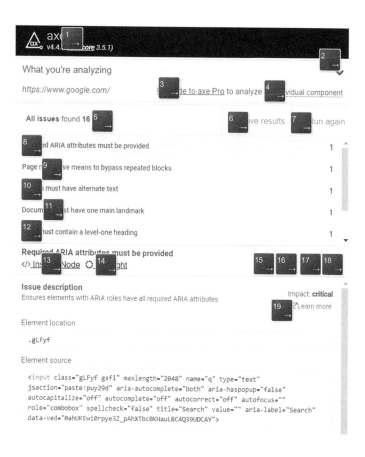

What you're analyzing

https://www.google.com/

Upgrade to axe Pro to analyze individual component

All **issues** found 16

Save results   Run again

Required ARIA attributes must be provided	1
Page must have means to bypass repeated blocks	1
Images must have alternate text	1
Document must have one main landmark	1
Page must contain a level-one heading	1

Required ARIA attributes must be provided

</> Inspect Node ○ Highlight

Issue description

Ensures elements with ARIA roles have all required ARIA attributes

Impact: **critical**

Learn more

Element location

.gLFyf

Element source

```
<input class="gLFyf gsfi" maxlength="2048" name="q" type="text"
jsaction="paste:puy29d" aria-autocomplete="both" aria-haspopup="false"
autocapitalize="off" autocomplete="off" autocorrect="off" autofocus=""
role="combobox" spellcheck="false" title="Search" value="" aria-label="Search"
data-ved="0ahUKEwi0rpye3Z_pAhXTbc0KHauLBC4Q39UDCAY">
```

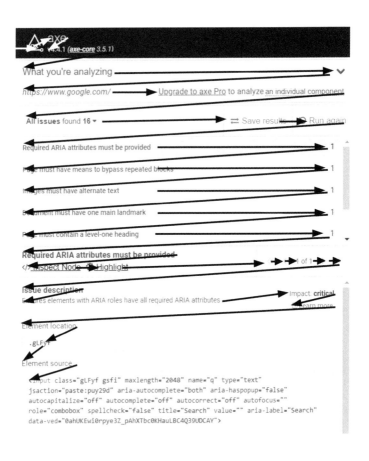

You will also notice that there is more content that is readable than the content that is focusable; this is important because keyboards and screen readers have different mechanisms for reading static content versus navigating-to and interacting-with interactive elements, so these two should be separated out very explicitly.

> **UPSIDE:** The first advantage of this approach is that the design comps provide input to both the test writers (whether developers write the tests or whether the test are written by a QA function) and the developers themselves. Developers use the information to choose the correct semantic elements and semantic markup, and the testers use them to validate these choices.

The second advantage of the process of thinking through all the roles, names, and interactions is that it can lead to the identification of what my colleague, Matt Isner, likes to call a "user-interface chimera."

A user-interface chimera is a UI design that is trying to be too many things at the same time. An example of this might be a menu item that is trying to serve as a control to open a sub-menu, and at the same time as a link that leads to a different page. While it is possible to use such a control with a mouse with mouseover logic, it is impossible to communicate the duplicate roles to a screen reader user, and the interaction mechanism for a keyboard is not intuitive. This means the functionality appears absent for some types of users. By going through the process of having to specify the role of the element, you have exposed the fact that it is acting as both a link and a menu item—leading to the realization that it is an accessibility and usability problem.

Thinking through the communication of the design intent can also identify designs that are very difficult to make accessible. This is often a "bail out," where the UI designer did not have enough time and/or information to make a better design decision, or it might simply be an example of the adoption of a common technology without much thought.

These chimeras and difficult designs offer the team an opportunity to design a better solution by asking, "What does the user want to do?" or "Why are we using this standard approach?" The end result of this process is often a solution that is more usable for everyone and completely accessible for people with disabilities.

> **WARNING:** This practice often changes the previous separation of duties between designers and developers. Designers may have been told in the past that it is not their role to tell developers how to implement features. In our opinion, it is not changing anything except clarifying requirements that were previously unstated. Developers do not have to use a `<button>` element to implement a UI component with a role of button, but if not, then they have to implement some of the functionality that a `<button>` element provides for free, including keyboard interaction, correct handling of enabled/disabled states, etc.

4.4 Practice: Create a User Interface Pattern Library

GOAL: Leverage accessible interaction designs, markup, and implementations across a large number of development teams while maintaining flexibility of implementation and look.

PRACTICE DESCRIPTION: Making applications accessible consists of paying attention to four high-level aspects of user interface design and implementation.

1. The color, font, iconography, and layout design choices that represent the roles, states, and values of the user interface elements across viewport sizes—**the look**;
2. The markup used to represent the names, roles, values, and states of the user interface elements—**the markup**;
3. The multi-input device interaction designs of the user interface components—**the interaction**; and
4. The implementation of the interactions and generation of the UI content—**the implementation.**

A pattern library is the definition of these four aspects where only the fourth aspect is dependent on the technology-specific framework or technology (within reason). This allows the implementing team to choose which aspects of the pattern they want to adopt and which aspects they need to adapt to their specific situation.

For example, if a team has adopted a new UI

development framework—say Vue.js—and the existing pattern library has implementations in React, then this team can take the look, the markup, and the specification for the interaction from the pattern library and implement these in Vue.

At a minimum, this eliminates accessibility issues because it clearly specifies the markup (and how that changes throughout all the different UI states and values) and the different modes of interaction with that component that support different devices and abilities. These are two very high-volume sources of custom component accessibility defects; by adopting the pattern library solutions, teams can avoid falling into these traps.

EXAMPLE: The Deque product user interfaces are all currently based on a pattern library called Cauldron (https://pattern-library.dequelabs.com/). At its base level, Cauldron specifies the look, the use, and the markup of the UI components. Building on top of this are the implementations in different technologies, including https://github.com/dequelabs/pattern-library and https://github.com/dequelabs/cauldron-react.

EXAMPLE: One of Deque's customers created a user interface widget library and had used it very extensively for a couple of years before they became aware of their accessibility requirements under the Accessibility for Ontarians with Disabilities Act. The widespread use of this component library was one of the major reasons the customer was able to become compliant within a reasonable time frame, because fixing a small number of components addressed 60% of the accessibility issues within their large portfolio of applications.

Your agile methodology might not allow you to develop a library like this ahead of time, but you can build one up over time, thereby reducing the effort necessary to develop and fix accessible components over time.

4.5 Practice: Leverage an Accessibility Automation Library

When developed by a team with little accessibility knowledge, our data shows that the average Web page averages twenty accessibility issues. Some surveys of a large numbers of sites claim that the number is as high as seventy defects per page. While mobile applications tend to have simpler views, a similar number of issues is to be expected over the course of an entire user workflow.

Automated testing of functionality saves time in development by allowing releases to happen more often. The same holds true for accessibility testing.

Writing automated tests takes time and effort, and there are a lot of additional assertions that need to be made when testing accessibility. Using an off-the-shelf automated accessibility testing library can save a large amount of time in the creation of an automated test suite.

Choose a library that generates zero false positives; this allows your tests to make assertions on the results, secure in the knowledge that if a test fails, the failure needs to be taken seriously. This, in turn, allows these tests to be embedded into continuous integration pipelines as checks that must be passed before code changes can be approved and merged.

Think about the ways that your developers work when fixing issues that are found in the automated tests and choose a tool that makes that easy. A tool should integrate into the browser or IDE's debugging environment and provide both an interactive testing mode (e.g., a browser extension) and an API that can be embedded into automated tests. A spider- or robot-like utility can also be very useful for teams that do not have full test coverage of all their UI states and/or functionality.

Studies that we have done on behalf of our large customers have shown that the use of these tools can eliminate 50% of the accessibility errors (by number of occurrences), eliminating a lot of cost from the development process by avoiding issues making it to later stages of the development cycle.

GOAL: Save time during development by eliminating all of the common accessibility defects that can be found through generic automation before the code makes it into the code base.

A side effect of this goal is an increase in the accessibility skills of the developers and testers who use the automated tool.

PRACTICE DESCRIPTION: Require developers to test all changed or new user interface states prior to submitting code to the repository. Integrate the execution of these tests into the build process on the continuous integration server, and include checks in your source code repository that do not allow changes to be merged if the tests fail.

This testing is best done by integrating the automation API calls into integration functional tests that test the new UI functionality, then asserting that the automation library returned zero accessibility errors.

When starting out, it is best to embed these API calls into all functional tests; however, with experience, teams will realize that there are subtle differences between functional testing and accessibility testing that might require the writing of specific tests to expose specific states of the user interface purely for accessibility. Also, many functional tests expose the same UI over and over, and it is only necessary to perform the accessibility testing on one iteration of each UI state.

EXAMPLE: The following code shows a React login form component accessibility unit test using Jest and Enzyme with JSDOM for emulating the browser DOM. This unit test is a small fraction of the unit tests covering all of the functionality of the component.

```
...
import axe from 'axe-core'

...
test('Form has no accessibility violations', (done) => {
    const fields = [ 'Dogs', 'Cats' ]
    const FormComponent = utils.mountToDoc(
        <LoginForm headline="Woof and hiss" fields={fields} />
    )
    const formNode = FormComponent.getDOMNode()
    axe.run(formNode, config)
        .then(({ violations }) => {
            if (violations.length) {
                const err = utils.printViolations(violations)
                done.fail(err)
            } else {
                done()
            }
        })
})
...
```

Note that the unit test mounts the component and obtains a DOM node in order to do the testing. This is because accessibility tests need to know the real display state of the DOM nodes in order to be able to determine what will be exposed to the assistive technologies and their users. Unit tests like this can cover about 80% of what generic libraries can test. The rest of the testing should occur on the complete assembled user interface. For this reason, we recommend integrating a library like this into integration (end-to-end) tests.

The following code shows how to use the axe-core testing library in an end-to-end test using Mocha and JavaScript Selenium.

```
const Selenium = require('selenium-webdriver'),
        AxeBuilder = require('axe-webdriverjs');
...
                    driver = new Selenium.Builder()
                      .forBrowser('chrome')
                              .build();
...
    it('should find no violations', function(done) {
        driver
            .findElement(Selenium.By.css('.App'))
          .then(function() {
            new AxeBuilder(driver)
              .analyze(function(results) {
              console.log(TestUtils.printViolations(results.violations));
                assert.equal(results.violations.length, 0);
                done();
              });
          });
    });
```

4.6 Practice: Automate Device and Assistive Technology Testing

Testing with assistive technologies and different input devices (like the keyboard) is expensive and time consuming. This means that in an agile environment, it will either slow down the process while also increasing expense, or it will not be done, leading to accessibility regressions.

While it is not currently possible to directly automate assistive technologies and write automated tests in a cross-platform way, it is possible to write tests that confirm the required markup and code that makes the assistive technologies work meet the requirements.

> **GOAL:** To ensure that implementations work with the set of assistive technologies required to meet the "accessibility supported" WCAG 2 requirement, while also leveraging automation for regression testing. This eliminates costly manual regression testing and allows faster, less expensive iterations that result in high quality, accessible code.

> **PRACTICE DESCRIPTION:** During development, have developers write specific tests to validate the conditions required to communicate name, role, value, and state to the assistive technologies, and ensure that these are correctly interpreted by the assistive technologies by performing tests using a representative set of assistive technologies, including at least one screen reader and a keyboard without a screen reader.

Of particular importance are tests for the alternative device interactions. A good example of this is the JavaScript handlers that are required to implement custom-component keyboard interactions. The tests should be written to include assertions on what happens as the user "interacts" with the UI. For example, if clicking a button should open a dialog and set focus into that dialog, then add assertions to test that.

Write tests that make assertions on the ARIA attribute and other state changes that should occur as a user "interacts" with the UI. These state changes should have corresponding changes to attributes and/or off-screen text that allow assistive technologies to expose the changed state, value, or name to users of assistive technologies.

Write tests that assert the expectations with respect to the order in which interactive components will be focused using TAB key navigation (Web) and write tests to assert the order in which content will be read by the user (Web and native mobile).

EXAMPLE: One of the components of accessibility testing which requires humans is the validation that the meaning conveyed by the visual user interface corresponds with the meaning conveyed through other senses, like voice. A simple example of this is validating that the alternative text of an image matches the image visuals. Websites often contain standard symbols and logos that appear in different locations. Simple assertions can be written to validate that the alternative texts for these graphics match the resource location. Doing this will ensure that if either the resource locator or the text changes, the test will alert the developer to check whether the text is still relevant and update the test.

EXAMPLE: The ARIA authoring guidelines provide a description of how widgets should behave when being used with different input devices. This includes keyboards. Much of this keyboard interaction can be tested in a fully automated fashion using keyboard event simulation.

When writing the code for a widget, developers are adding the appropriate markup and event handlers and writing assertions for these. At various points during this process, when testing with the mouse and/or touch, the developers should test the functionality using a screen reader and a keyboard to ensure that the state changes and other information are announced correctly and that the event handlers work correctly with a screen reader and without one. Changes are encoded into the tests. This functionality then only needs to be tested manually if the code changes, or the supported set of assistive technologies changes.

The following code snippet shows ARIA markup validation for the implementation of an ARIA menu widget. This example has been lifted from the a11yfy library and shortened for brevity. The full source code is available on Github at https://github.com/dylanb/a11yfy.

```
…
test("That the markup of the menu is applied correctly", function () {
    var $menu = jQuery("#menu-test-1"),
        $topMenuItems;
    expect(16);
    $menu.a11yfy("menu");
    $topMenuItems = $menu.find(">li[role='menuitem']");
```

```
    equal($menu.attr("role"), "menubar", "top ul should have role menubar");
     ok($menu.hasClass("allyfy-top-level-menu"), "should have to level
menu class");
   $topMenuItems.each(function(index, value) {
        if (index === 0) {
            equal(jQuery(value).attr("tabindex"), "0",
                                "the first top level menu item should be
focusable");
        } else {
            equal(jQuery(value).attr("tabindex"), "-1",
                                "All other top level menu items should not
be focusable");
        }
    });
    equal($menu.find(">li.allyfy-has-submenu").length, 2,
                    "There should be two top level menu items with sub
menus");
    equal(jQuery($topMenuItems[1]).attr("aria-haspopup"), "true",
                    "The second top level menu item should have an aia-
haspopup attribute of true");
   equal(jQuery($topMenuItems[1]).find("li.allyfy-has-submenu")
                    .attr("aria-haspopup"), "true",
                    "The sub-submenu item must also have aria-haspopup
true");
});

…
```

4.7 Practice: Manage Accessibility Defects Systematically

Many accessibility experts have expectations about the quality of software that are out of sync with the reality of software development. While we all strive for defect-free software and implement practices like test driven development (TDD) to try to achieve this, defects are a fact that we have to manage. Accessibility defects are no different, and they should be managed in a very similar way.

In one aspect, accessibility defects are quite different from functional defects: Organizations that sell software to the US Federal Government and related institutions are required to produce a document that lists all the known accessibility defects in the form of a Voluntary Product Accessibility Template (VPAT). In the world of waterfall software development, the VPAT production process involved a comprehensive accessibility audit, which is incompatible with agile practices.

GOAL: Implement an accessibility defect management policy that allows for the consistent prioritization of accessibility issues in ways that mirror the prioritization of other classes of defects, and produce and maintain an accurate and complete VPAT with each release in an agile manner.

PRACTICE DESCRIPTION: There are two components to this practice:

1. Creating and implementing a way to evaluate the impact of an accessibility issue and assigning it a priority that matches the equivalent defect priority for other functional and non-functional defects; and

2. Maintaining a defect management system where every accessibility defect is identifiable along with the other relevant VPAT information, allowing the defect management system to be used to generate the VPAT as a release artifact.

Not all accessibility defects are created equal: A missing alternative text for an image can be a blocker for a blind user if that image is part of an image button required to complete the main business flow of a Web application, or it could be a minor inconvenience if it is a social icon in the footer of the page. This should underpin the priority system assigned to any accessibility defect. If the organization has defect priorities that are used to determine ship/no-ship, then the accessibility impact should be mapped to these. The table following is an example accessibility-prioritization-table with mappings to the standard actions the organization takes for comparable functional defects.

Your team should map these actions onto your processes in such a way that the intent is maintained.

Accessibility Priority	Criteria for Assignment
Critical	The issue affects at least one disability such that a critical business function cannot be used by a user with an affected disability. Think about the impact from this perspective: If all users could not use this functionality, would we consider that critical?
Serious	The issue affects at least one disability such that critical business functionality can only be used with an acceptable workaround; or The issue affects functionality that is not essential, but prevents at least one disability from being able to use this functionality.

Action

Stop deployment/release of affected software until the defect is remediated. If the defect is discovered in production, implement a hot fix immediately. If the hot fix cannot be implemented immediately, create an alternative channel for achieving the functionality and train support and call center staff on how to direct users to the alternative channel.

Fix the defect in the very next deployment/release. Publish documentation on the workaround and train support and call center staff on how to deal with the issue. If the defect is discovered in production, update the VPAT to reflect the newly discovered defect.

Accessibility Priority	Criteria for Assignment
Moderate	The issue affects functionality that is not essential and has an acceptable workaround.
Minor	The issue affects functionality in a distracting way (e.g., duplicate accessible names, presentational elements that are not marked as presentational, or inconsistent use of markup).

This triage and assignment obviously require judgement; so, how do automatically-generated issues get assigned priorities? In the axe-core library, we take the following approach: If the defect could affect a particular disability in such a way that could be a blocker of essential functionality, then we assign it an impact of "critical." We

Action

Publish documentation on the workaround. Train support and call center staff on how to deal with the issue. If the defect is discovered in production, update the VPAT.

Assign defect fix priority in a similar way to defects that affect general site usability.

If the defect is discovered in production, update the VPAT.

Assign defect fix priority in a similar way to defects that affect brand, consistency of use, and look-and-feel.

expect a human to review this default decision and downgrade it if applicable. You could take a similar approach in your automated tests, but you also likely know whether the affected functionality is essential and make more nuanced decisions.

In agile development, the backlog should represent the complete state of all known defects as well as the current best understanding of planned future improvements. If your team is implementing this well and layering the defect prioritization process described above on top of it, then you should be able to generate at any point in time a complete list of all known defects. By meeting a few criteria (some of which may be new), your existing practice will allow you to generate a complete list of all known accessibility defects for any given release with enough information to generate a VPAT from it. (Note: I have included the requirements for generating the WCAG 2.1 VPAT; similar but slightly different requirements need to be met if generating one of the other variants of this document. See https://www.itic.org/policy/accessibility/vpat for details on all the variants and for the document templates for all variants.)

1. Ensure that part of your definition of "done" for any ticket includes accessibility testing (see the relevant practices above);

2. Ensure that bugs can be tagged with:

   i.   A tag that identifies them as affecting accessibility;
   ii. A set of tags that identify which WCAG success criteria are affected;
   iii. A short description of the way the defect affects people with disabilities;
   iv. The version(s) affected;
   v.   The version(s) where the defect was first fixed; and
   vi. The open/closed (or equivalent) status.

3. Implement a process that ensures that all of the above tags and statuses are created, maintained, and reviewed for accuracy and quality.

   Whenever a release is "cut," a query can be applied to the defect management system to generate all known "open" accessibility issues that affect that release. This includes all the information required to generate or edit the VPAT template for that release.

4.8 Practice: Measure Accessibility

Adopting accessible development practices is no different than any other organizational change initiative. It requires the adoption of a lot of new practices, new skills, and changes to existing practices. Teams should be encouraged to improve incrementally over time with realistic and achievable goals that can be measured and celebrated.

> **GOAL:** Reinforce the change in practices and skills and motivate the teams to continue to improve.
>
> **PRACTICE DESCRIPTION:** Break accessibility into milestones with achievable, measurable goals. Have

each successive milestone build on the previous ones towards the final goal of a sustainable development process that produces accessible applications.

Have accessibility coaches perform spotcheck audits on content and produce reports for retrospectives with the intent of celebrating wins and identifying opportunities for improvement. An example of a set of progressive milestones is:

1. Achieve a state where all code is clean of all issues that can be found with a generic automated accessibility testing tool;

2. Achieve a state where the meaning of all states, names, values, and roles of all the content are being correctly exposed to assistive technologies and tested automatically;

3. Achieve a state where all interactive elements are comprehensively tested with the keyboard and assistive technologies, and the regression testing is automated; and

4. Achieve 100% accessible content and functionality.

Breaking the milestones up further into ones that cover new functionality first and existing code and functionality later is another technique for making them smaller and easier to achieve.

With a set of milestones, it is possible to create metrics that measure the progress towards them in a way that makes sense for the team. Examples of metrics that match the milestones above are:

1. Percentage of designs that have used inclusive personas and included accessibility markup;
2. Percentage of UI code with a generic accessibility library integrated into the automated tests; and
3. Percentage of new features that meet the current standard for accessibility at release.

Another good practice is to measure the team's maturation process:

1. Coach has gained the trust of the team;
2. Developer, designer, and BSA training completion; and
3. Frequency of use of tools.

Put in place technologies that allow these metrics to be gathered and tracked, and publish the results in a location that is prominent and visible to the whole team (physical and/or virtual).

4.9 Practice: Include Accessibility in Retrospectives and Sprint Planning

Early in the transformation to agile accessibility, team members will not be proficient in the skills and the practices required; they will have to take action to support the learning and improvement process.

> **GOAL:** To reinforce the adoption of agile accessibility and allow the team to improve their accessibility practices and skills.

PRACTICE DESCRIPTION: Include accessibility coaches in the sprint retrospective meetings. Have the accessibility coaches bring the most up-to-date accessibility metrics and their spot check results to the meeting and foster discussion amongst the team about areas that are either not improving or which may have regressed.

Reserve time on the agenda for discussing accessibility practices and the accessibility skills of team members. Seek open discussion on instances where the skills or practices were well-implemented and where they were either forgotten or did not work well. Identify opportunities for additional coaching, skills training, or tools to help improve outcomes.

During sprint planning, have the team members brainstorm the accessibility impacts of the stories that are being proposed and also identify complex interactions, new widgets, or other novel functionality that might require either input from an accessibility coach or additional research. Encourage team members to think about the impact of accessibility on the story points and the team's overall velocity.

Putting It Together

It might seem obvious to you at this point, but it is worth stating: These practices, when applied, will result in accessibility becoming an integral part of your software development process. The key point is that accessibility is only scalable, affordable, and sustainable when it is fully integrated into all aspects of the software ideation and development process.

Getting from where you currently are to where you need to be requires change. This change will not happen if it is not acknowledged and explicitly managed. Some of the practices help with implementing and managing that change explicitly.

Getting from where you are to where you need to be requires learning new skills. Some of the practices are, in themselves, new skills that need to be learned and developed. Some of the practices help support the learning process.

Some practices are very technical and practical in that they help with the specifics of implementation. Some practices help with user experience: Empathy, design, and measuring the outcomes as experienced by users.

Some practices help to ensure the quality of new features, user interfaces, and code; some practices help to ensure that this quality is maintained over the lifetimes of these artifacts.

Finally, some practices help with one of the foundations of agile software development—communication.

All of the practices help to inject accessibility into the process at the earliest point possible. By implementing them, you will have shifted your accessibility activities as far "left" in your process as possible. This will drive down the costs and drive up the results.

I look forward to learning from you as you travel on this journey. Please send me your feedback on Twitter @dylanbarrell or via email dylan@barrell.com.

Glossary of Terms

This book is written to be used by agile team members as well as people working in or managing the central accessibility team. This glossary translates common terms used by one of these groups for the benefit of the other.

ADA (Americans with Disabilities Act): US Federal legislation that aims to protect the rights of people with disabilities.

API (Application Programming Interface): a mechanism for one piece of software to interact, programmatically, with another piece of software.

ARIA (Accessible Rich Internet Applications): a W3C standard specification for additional markup that can be applied to languages like HTML to add accessibility information that is not possible with standard HTML.

BSA (Business Systems Analyst): a common role within development teams; while the exact definition of the role will differ from organization to organization, the BSA is generally responsible for specifying the business and end-user requirements of stories and setting priorities.

Comp (Comprehensive Layout): a visual layout that is a draft of what the application's user interface will look like. Comps are used in many forms of creative design, including software user interface design.

DOM (Document Object Model): the manifestation of an HTML Web page with the browser that allows for programmatic access to inspect and manipulate the Web page. Dynamic Web applications manipulate the DOM to implement the changes in content and appearance that users see.

IDE (Integrated Development Environment): an editor with other tools integrated that makes developing, testing, and fixing software more efficient.

JIRA: a system that is used to track and manage bugs, enhancement requests, tasks, tickets, and many other types of work related to software development.

JSDOM: an implementation of the DOM APIs in JavaScript that does not include the full functionality of a browser. It is used in automated testing environments because it is more lightweight than a full browser.

Minimally Viable Designs, or **Minimally Viable Product:** these are product designs and definitions that minimize the amount of software that has to be written while at the same time providing enough value that the product can be commercially viable.

Persona: a fictitious character created by user experience designers to inspire the design of exceptional user experiences for the intended target user base. They are intended to allow the designers to really understand who they are designing products for.

Sprint: a period of time between one and three weeks, during which an agile team will develop a series of features, improvements, and bug fixes for release at the end of the sprint. Tends to be used by agile teams following the SCRUM methodology.

Sprint Retrospective: a meeting that occurs at the end of every sprint where the team members discuss what went well, what did not, and brainstorm ideas for how they can improve the processes to eliminate the recurrence of the things that did not go well. It is designed to foster the culture of continuous improvement.

TDD (Test Driven Development): a practice whereby software is developed by first writing the automated tests for the functionality and then implementing that functionality and validating that it passes the tests.

WCAG (Web Content Accessibility Guidelines): a series of W3C standards that specify the requirements for applications to meet in order for these to meet certain accessibility levels. WCAG 2 is the most commonly used version of this standard.

UI (User Interface): the user interface is any component of the system that takes user input and provides output to the user. For the most part, user interfaces are implemented on some sort of flat-screen device, but virtual reality goggles, voice input, and gestures are becoming more common forms of input and output.

UX (User Experience): generally refers to the practice of creating great experiences for users as they encounter the company and its offerings.

While the practice is often broader than just software, many teams' abilities to influence the overall experience are restricted to their specific software component or application.

VPAT (Voluntary Product Accessibility Template): a standard format for reporting on the accessibility of a specific software product and how it was tested for accessibility. It is required by all US Federal agencies when they purchase software, but is gaining traction outside of this domain.

Issue Prevention Opportunity

WCAG 2.0 Success Criteria (A & AA)	UX/UI Design	Coding	Automated Testing
1.1.1 Non-text Content	Strong	Moderate	Moderate
1.3.1 Info and Relationships	Strong	Strong	Moderate
1.3.2 Meaningful Sequence	Strong	Strong	None
1.3.3 Sensory Characteristics	Strong	None	None

WCAG 2.0 Success Criteria (A & AA)	UX/UI Design	Coding	Automated Testing
1.4.1 Use of Color	Strong	None	None
1.4.2 Audio Control	Strong	None	None
1.4.3 Contrast (Minimum)	Strong	None	Strong
1.4.4 Resize text	None	Strong	None
1.4.5 Images of Text	Strong	Moderate	None
2.1.1 Keyboard	Strong	Strong	Weak
2.1.2 No Keyboard Trap	None	Strong	None
2.2.1 Timing Adjustable	Strong	None	Weak
2.2.2 Pause, Stop, Hide	Strong	None	Weak

WCAG 2.0 Success Criteria (A & AA)	UX/UI Design	Coding	Automated Testing
2.3.1 Three Flashes or Below Threshold	Strong	None	None
2.4.1 Bypass Blocks	Strong	Strong	Moderate
2.4.2 Page Titled	Strong	Moderate	Strong
2.4.3 Focus Order	Strong	Strong	None
2.4.4 Link Purpose (In Context)	Moderate	None	None
2.4.5 Multiple Ways	Moderate	None	None
2.4.6 Headings and Labels	Moderate	Moderate	None
2.4.7 Focus Visible	Strong	Moderate	None
3.1.1 Language of Page	None	Strong	Strong

WCAG 2.0 Success Criteria (A & AA)	UX/UI Design	Coding	Automated Testing
3.1.2 Language of Parts	None	Strong	Weak
3.2.1 On Focus	Strong	Moderate	None
3.2.2 On Input	Strong	Moderate	None
3.2.3 Consistent Navigation	Strong	None	None
3.2.4 Consistent Identification	Strong	None	None
3.3.1 Error Identification	Strong	Moderate	None
3.3.2 Labels or Instructions	Strong	Moderate	None
3.3.3 Error Suggestion	Strong	None	None

WCAG 2.0 Success Criteria (A & AA)	UX/UI Design	Coding	Automated Testing
3.3.4 Error Prevention (Legal, Financial, Data)	Strong	None	None
4.1.1 Parsing	None	Strong	Strong
4.1.2 Name, Role, Value	Strong	Strong	Moderate

Acknowledgments

I would like to thank everyone who made it possible for me to write this book.

Thank you to those who reviewed and gave me feedback on the early drafts. Special thanks to Camron Shimy from Google, who was particularly insightful and gave me ideas that led to the chapter on defect management.

Denis Boudreau provided inspiration on the personas and also provided the image of Lucy.

Ben Allen gave thoughtful feedback that helped to clarify many sections.

Thanks to my colleagues, Chris McMeeking,

Noah Mashni, and Keith Rhodes, for feedback that helped me improve the book in many ways.

Thank you to Anik Ganguly, who introduced me to Deque Systems and therefore to accessibility. Thank you for your feedback on this book and your mentoring, inspiration, and encouragement for the many years I have had the privilege to work with you.

Thank you to Preety Kumar for the opportunity she has afforded all of us at Deque, for her vision that created the company, and for her leadership in the accessibility field.

Thank you to all my colleagues at Deque who inspire me every day and without whom this work would not be possible.

Last but not least, I would like to thank my wife Karin for giving me the time and the space to work on this book at night and on the weekends, and for checking my proofs and arguing with me about the correct grammar for colons, lists, and many other finer points—all of which ultimately improved the quality of this book.